You Promised Me, God!

Donald L. Deffner

Publishing House
St. Louis

Photo credits:
Cover—Wunder from Three Lions; 18—Fishback of Alpha; 27—
Josef Muench; 34—Walt Disney Productions; 42—Joan E. Rahn;
49—Hallinan of FPG; 64—Ray Atkeson; 72—Wendler of FPG; 80—
Robert Holland

Concordia Publishing House, St. Louis, Missouri
Copyright © 1981 Concordia Publishing House
MANUFACTURED IN THE UNITED STATES OF AMERICA

Library of Congress Cataloging in Publication Data

Deffner, Donald L
        You promised me, God!

        1. God—Promises—Meditations. I. Title.
BT180.P7D43   231.7   80-25256
ISBN 0-570-03827-8 (pbk.)

To my wife,
Corinne

Author's Preface

Often the Christian feels that God is silent or isn't even there any longer. But the God who cannot lie has promised His faithfulness to us. And there are nearly 9,000 promises of God in the Scriptures. While we may imagine God doesn't know what's going on in our lives or care about us, the real problem often is that we don't believe the mighty promises of God. As James puts it: "You do not have what you want because you do not ask God for it" James 4:2 TEV.

Yet our hope is not in the promises of God but in the Promiser Himself. Accordingly, an additional difficulty we often have in growing as Christians is that we fail to understand the true nature of the Promiser and the ways in which He works with us. We live with a conception of God which we have devised by ourselves—and that's where our predicament begins.

It is necessary to go back to the Scriptures again and again and search out the true God. We find throughout the Old and New Testaments that God never desires the misery or the death of His children. There we find One who is just and loving, chastising and patient, seemingly silent at times and yet always true to His promises. He says that when we call on Him He will answer, but in His own way and at His own time.

Knowing these many aspects of God's character, as He has described Himself in Scripture, helps us to learn how to mature in our relationship with Him. In meditating on what God is like and on what He has promised us, we are guided by the Holy Spirit to learn how to pray, how to live, and how to die.

In the following vignettes I have sought to be faithful to the nature of God as revealed in the Old and New Testaments. Each piece is based on Scripture passages listed in the order they are alluded to in the vignette. Where a number (1) appears with a vignette it corresponds to the author listed at the end who is to be credited for the statement(s) or germinal ideal behind the piece.

May the Holy Spirit bless your meditations on these promises from our Lord, that you may grow stronger in reliance on the One who made them—the Promiser Himself.

How This Book Can Be Used

What goes on in the mind of God all day? What are His "feelings" when His children doubt Him, think He seems so remote and silent, and when He doesn't seem to respond to their pain or despair?

Scripture affirms that we cannot comprehend the mind of God (Romans 11:23; 1 Corinthians 2:16) or predict what actions He is going to take at what time. But we *do* have the *promises* of God—and they are sure.

For every Christian it is going to be different—discovering the fulfillment of God's promises to each person in His own unique way.

Beyond using this little volume for personal devotions, another possibility would be for a small group of people to read each vignette, then the Scripture passages in a variety of translations, and afterwards each person might share how this particular promise of God has been evidenced in his or her life. Group participants may also want to add other relevant Scripture passages which come to mind.

And then . . . why not write some yourself?

Contents

The Christian asks—
Why am I so afraid, God? God responds—

The Christian asks—
What else do I need to hear, God? God responds—

THE CHRISTIAN ASKS—

Where were You when I needed You, God?

GOD RESPONDS—

A Way of Escape

You think
you're not going to make it
The test will be
more than you can bear
But I promise you
I will not give you
more than you can handle
As your days are
so shall your strength be
Underneath you will be
My everlasting arms
so don't be dismayed
I am your God
I will strengthen you
I will help you
I will hold you up
with My strong right hand
or My Name isn't God
Don't worry in advance
of the test

for I won't give you the fare
for your journey
ahead of time
but just when
you need it
1 Corinthians 10:13   Deuteronomy 33:25, 27
Isaiah 41:10

Did You See Me?

Did you see Me today?
I was there
I peeked through your curtain
with a golden sunbeam
as you awoke
I blew on your cheek
as you walked outside
I whispered to you
in the trees
I waved at you
with a flower
I cried for you
with that afternoon shower
I sang to you
in the cries and calls
of the birds
Did you hear Me?
Feel Me?
Oh, taste and see
that I am good
and spread My gifts
around you
on the earth

But the best
is yet
to come
Psalm 34:8

Hanging Around the Altar

You said you sought Me
but didn't find Me
Maybe you've just been
hanging around the altar
for many years
going through the motions
in worship.
And if the enemy appeared
you would tell him that
though you were a church member
you'd really been on his side
all the time!
Do you seek Me?
I do not delight
in casual acquaintance
When you truly seek Me
with all your heart
you will surely find Me
That's a promise
Proverbs 8:17   Proverbs 8:35   Jeremiah 29:13

What Shall I Call Him?

Remember that stranger
you entertained
the other day
and haven't seen since?
That may have been
one of My angels
just checking you out
But I have another
promise for you
Even as little children
have specific angels
up here in My presence
so one of My angels protects you
every day
so you don't get hurt
Concentrate on that
In fact
why don't you
give your angel
a name?
Hebrews 13:2   Matthew 18:10   Matthew 4:6

Prayer

O Lord, forgive me for doubting Your love
and care. Keep me mindful that even when You
are silent, You are still there. Help me to see the
many signs of Your presence and providence all
around me every day. In the strong name of Jesus
Christ. Amen.

THE CHRISTIAN ASKS—

Why don't You come down and talk to me, God?

GOD RESPONDS—

You're Not Listening

Sometimes
I try to talk to you
but you are asking Me
so many questions
you don't wait
for My answer
Be still,
and know
that I
am God
Psalm 46:10

Are You Disconnected?

Sometimes
you wonder where
I went

Maybe
you're not plugged in
to My Word
and Sacraments
I don't come
in one great big zap
out of the blue
I work through means
tools channels and hookups
So next time
don't look for Me
in a vacuum
Make sure you're connected
to My Word
To your baptism and the Eucharist
And then My power
will flow
into you
Romans 10:17

Not on Your Own

When the testing time comes
don't make the mistake
of depending on your own power
to make it through in
overcoming temptation
Bearing up
and holding on
being able to last out the pain
is not a conscious act
of your own will
but of My power in you

Don't push yourself
into loneliness or despair or failure
by the mistake of self-dependence
when the trial approaches
Focus on Me
I am the source of your strength
You are not
We're in your testing together
Concentrate
on that
1 Corinthians 10:13   Psalm 50:15   Hebrews 12:2

Unanswered Prayers

Do you want to know why
you didn't get the answers
you wanted to those prayers?
One time you thought you knew more
than I did
You arranged on your own
to get what you wanted
That wasn't a valid prayer
Another time you tried to get
My support
for your own idea
To pray was correct
but your goal was unworthy
Another time you tried to
condition My will
to the way you
wanted things to be
Another time you prayed
but then did nothing

Don't depend just on praying
but depend on Me
My will
And at times you will discover
the blessing
of getting an answer
you never expected
James 4:3   Deuteronomy 3:23-27
John 16:23-24   Matthew 26:39

Prayer

O great and wonderful God, keep me from thinking I'm on my own in my Christian walk. Remind me always to stay actively within the channels of Your grace through Word and Sacrament. Keep my eyes ever focused not on myself, but on my Savior, Jesus Christ. In His strong name I pray. Amen.

THE CHRISTIAN ASKS—

Don't You care, God?

GOD RESPONDS—

After the Party

I saw you at the party
Wit poured from your lips
People laughed at you
and admired you
You were the center of attention
but you went home
and wanted to kill yourself
I know the aches of your heart
You don't need to pretend with Me
I care for you
I really do
Put your burden on My shoulder
and I will carry it for you
all the way to Calvary
and beyond
1 Peter 5:7

I Saw You Fearful

I saw the beads of perspiration on your forehead
the panic in your heart

the fear tightening your fingers
I felt your terror
for I too was human—like you
I agonized in a garden one night
I sweat as though it were great drops of blood
I know distress
and pain
So do not be afraid
I am with you
I will not leave you comfortless
Remember
I am still in control
There is no panic
in heaven
Isaiah 41:10

The Three Gifts

I haven't heard you
say "Thank You" recently
Have you forgotten
that it is I who made you
and not you yourself?
That was gift
number one
Life itself
Don't you remember
My second gift?
Forgiveness
through My Son Jesus Christ
Forgiveness
for the misuse of
My life

24

lived in you
When did you last
say "Thank You"
for the third gift?
The freedom to
reject Me
You are not a puppet
an automaton
I do not force you
to love Me
But I do love you
I gave My all for you
What will you give to me?
"Thank You"?
Psalm 100:3   John 1:3   1 Corinthians 15:57

Life-lines

Don't ever think
I am so great or distant
or that there are so many
millions of people in the world
that I don't care personally
just for you
Remember the day
My Son said that
a shepherd searches for
the one lost sheep
the woman for
one lost coin
And when *you* were found
the angels up here rejoiced
I'll never forget you

Your name is written
in the Lamb's Book of Life
I have purchased you
You are etched
on the palms of My hands
You are Mine!

Ephesians 4:6   Luke 15:4-10
Revelation 3:5   Isaiah 49:16

Your Heart's Desires

Do you really believe
that I know
what is best for you?
That though you see only
the tangled side
of the tapestry
I see the other side
a beautiful, completed pattern
Do you really believe
that I know
what is best for you?
If you will but put
your hands in Mine
and trust Me—
commit yourself—
I will give you
your heart's desires
Not "what your heart desires "
But I will put
the right desires
into your heart
Do you really believe

that I know
what is best for you?

Matthew 9:28   John 11:27
John 16:31   Psalm 37:4-5

Consider the Sparrow

Did you just see
that bird
fly by?
My Son once said
a sparrow doesn't fall
to the ground
but that I am aware of it
That's true
Nothing escapes
My attention
If I so take care of
My creatures
and garb the earth
and order the galaxies
will I not take care
of you
My beloved?

Matthew 10:29-31   Matthew 6:28-34

Weeping at the Funeral

You thought I was
dead
because I was silent

or because I didn't act
to prevent that great disaster
or all the other suffering
and evil in the world?
I don't have to give you
an answer
except that
I AM GOD
and will not remain
forever silent
So don't weep
for Me
but weep
for yourself
and know that
I do care [5]
Luke 23:28

Prayer

O patient Lord, forgive me when I wallow in
self-centeredness. Give me the grace always to
remember how Christ also took my sins of self-
pity and self-indulgence upon Himself at Calvary, how He cared for me —to the very end—
dying in my stead. Thanks and praise be to You,
O most gracious God! You know what is best for
me today. Help me to believe that—and to live it.
In the strong name of Jesus Christ. Amen.

THE CHRISTIAN ASKS—

Why am I so lonely, God?

GOD RESPONDS—

Suicide

Don't think
you're alone
in contemplating
ending it all
It's not a new idea
even among Christians
But your life
is not your own
It is My life
lived in you
I know
your appointed time
But don't despair
I will give you
power
by the hour
to endure
or My name
isn't
God
1 Corinthians 6:19-20   1 John 4:15-16
Deuteronomy 33:25   Isaiah 41:10

The Tug of the Kite

You are really going to enjoy it
up here
I know that now
it's only like a dim image
in a mirror
But one day it will be
face to face
Now your knowledge
is limited
then it will be
complete
Do you feel
My tug at times?
That's your faith in Me
Like feeling the pull
of a kite
out of sight
I know you're caught
from both sides
to stay
or to be with Me
Stay, for now
Do My work
while it is day
before the night comes
Then you will be
always
with Me
1 Corinthians 13:12   Philippians 1:21-26

Love Me!

You've been pleading
for others to love you?
Do you want
a surprise?
If you would
show your love
to those around you
you would receive
more love
in return
than you
can imagine
Matthew 22:39   Luke 6:38   Galatians 6:9

The Bread of Sorrows

Why do you insist
on eating
the bread of sorrows
when you know
I want you to be
happy?
Here is the secret
Praise Me
and don't stop
praising Me
no matter what
your situation
for then I will come
to you
and lighten your heart

Praise Me
Praise Me
Praise Me
And My peace will come
and fill
your mind
Psalm 127:2   1 Thessalonians 5:18
Colossians 3:15   Philippians 4:7

Prayer

Faithful God, when I am lonely remind me how Your Son was lonely, too—especially on the cross. Give me, I pray, the ability to praise You in the midst of the most trying circumstances. By Your power enable me to do that which I cannot do alone. In the strong name of Jesus Christ. Amen.

THE CHRISTIAN ASKS—

Why are You so silent, God?

GOD RESPONDS—

A Silent God

You thought
I really didn't care
because you didn't hear Me
saying anything
You even wondered if
I existed any more.
But remember
I have always been
and always will be
I don't change
in My love for you
The fact that
I am silent at times
does not prove I am not there
Rather it is the silence *of*
your Creator
The absence of evidence
is not
the evidence
of absence
Psalm 14:1

Wait!

I know
you get very impatient
with Me
at times
But My plan for you
is good
It will move you
towards the goal
of true maturity
Meanwhile
I ask you to wait
for My plan
When you do
I promise you
I will renew your strength
The problem is
if you're not willing
to wait
for My way
you're not going
to have
your strength
renewed
Psalm 27:14   Romans 12:2   Isaiah 40:31

New Every Morning

Maybe you thought
that I had deserted you
but though you
did not see Me

I was there
Like the sun
cannot be seen
for a while
but is always shining
and returns each morning
so My love for you
never ceases
and My mercies are new
every morning
Let My bright beams
lighten your heart
for I assure you
I will never fail you
nor forsake you
That's a promise
1 Peter 1:8   Lamentations 3:22-23
Psalm 139:18   Joshua 1:5

Try Me and See

Your problem
is not
that I don't know
what's going on in your life
or that I don't care for you
You know I do
But your problem
is that you
don't really believe
My promises
It's as simple
as that

Try Me
and see
Mark 9:23   Mark 11:24   James 2:4

Satan Never Sleeps

He's always there
to tempt you
in a million different ways
even when you sleep
in the fantasy world
of your subconscious
But I overcame him
for you.
I met his tests
three times
in the person of
My Son
I promise you
the same victory is yours
through faith in Him
So remember that although
Satan never sleeps
I don't
either
Matthew 4:1-11   1 John 5:4   Psalm 121:4

The Right Timing

Remember that time
at the wedding at Cana

when My Son told His mother
His time had not yet come?
Keep that in mind
for My plans
are not necessarily
your plans
I know
what is best for you
and when I am ready
it will be
perfect timing
In the Name
of the Father
and of the Son
and the Holy Surprises

John 2:4   Isaiah 55:8   Jeremiah 29:11   John 7:6
Psalm 25:4   Psalm 27:11   Psalm 86:11

Believing is Seeing

You say
"Show me and I'll believe "
I say
"Believe in Me
and I'll show you "
Remember how My Son
told people it was their faith
that released His power
When you don't
believe in Me
you will find Me
strangely silent
But believe first,

and you will see
My power
Indeed, more signs and wonders
than you could ever
have expected
In fact
you'll be doing
greater things
than I did
Myself [2]

Mark 6:5-6	Matthew 8:13	Matthew 17:20
Mark 2:5-12	Mark 5:24-35	Luke 23:8-9
Mark 15:32	John 14:12	

Prayer

O majestic and wondrous God, give me, I pray, a true sense of awe at Your ways, ever believing—though not always seeing—that You know what is best for me. Move me to walk by faith and not by sight. In the strong name of Jesus Christ. Amen.

THE CHRISTIAN ASKS—

Do You really love me, God?

GOD RESPONDS—

I Love You

I love you
and there's nothing
you can do
to make Me stop
I love you
in spite of
what you have done
to Me
I love you
not because you
have loved Me
for I love you
though you are
a sinner
Not that you should
sin more
that grace
may abound
I love you
and because
I love you
now

you can still
be a sinner
and enjoy
the grace
of God [3]
John 4:10   Romans 6:1, 15

Thinking about You

Do you wonder sometimes
what I am thinking
about you?
Well, let Me tell you
I know the thoughts
that I think towards you
thoughts of peace
and not of evil
You are My child
I have redeemed you
I have called you
by your name
You are graven
on the palms of My hands
You are Mine
That's what I think
about you
Jeremiah 29:11   Isaiah 43:1   Isaiah 49:16

Unfailing

The stars never fail
to reflect their light

from aeons ago
do they?
There are some things
you can count on
including Me
the Maker
of all things
Now one day
all things will pass away
There will be a new heaven
and a new earth
But I and My promises
will never pass away
You can count
on that

Isaiah 40:8   Matthew 24:35
1 Peter 1:23   Revelation 21:1

What You Really Need

Sometimes you think
I love others more
than you?
Because they have certain gifts
talents, possessions
or the absence of woes and worries
unlike you
But be assured
I love you
as much as anyone else
in the whole world
Count your blessings
physical and spiritual

great and small
Believe now
that I will supply all your needs
Not what you think you need
but what I know
is best for you
And learn
in whatsoever state
you are in
to be content
I know that's hard
but I will give you the strength
to do it
That's a promise
John 3:16   Philippians 4:19   Psalm 37:4-5
Philippians 4:11   1 Corinthians 10:13

Take It Easy

I know how hard
you have been working
to earn your daily bread
I labored too
and then rested
after six days of creation
My Son
labored as a carpenter
until the day another labored
to help Him
carry His cross
When the
drudgery of toil
gets you down

come to Me
and I will give you
rest
But, meanwhile, labor
not for those things
which pass away
but for those things
which endure
One Day
you will enjoy rest
from your hard work
and the food that lasts
will be yours

Genesis 2:2   Matthew 13:55   Mark 15:21
Matthew 11:28   John 6:27   1 Corinthians 15:58
Revelation 14:13

Prayer

Lord, never let me doubt Your love, a love that pursued me even when I rejected it, and a love that sought me in spite of my not being loving! In the strong name of Jesus Christ. Amen.

THE CHRISTIAN ASKS—

Don't You see what I've been doing, God?

GOD RESPONDS—

Out of Breath?

Slow down!
Maybe you should
take down that plaque
that says
"Keep me going, Lord"
and put up the one saying
"Slow me down, Lord "
Let your mind and spirit
catch up with your body
Learn from My Son
to take time
for rest and meditation
Slow down!
Because great works of art
music, sculpture, writing
were not given to the world
by persons
out of breath
Psalm 23:2   Matthew 14:23   Luke 10:27

47

The Shape I'm In

Don't let the world
around you
squeeze you
into its own mold
but rather let Me
shape you
from within
Remember, your life
lived in this world
is actually My life
lived
in you
Romans 12:2   1 John 4:15-16

Stewards

I don't expect you to be
successful
effective
or superior to others
in all you do
But I do expect
faithfulness
in the use of your gifts
such as they are.
That means your abilities
and your limitations
That takes
some of the pressure off
doesn't it?
1 Corinthians 4:2

Prayer

Lord, keep reminding me not to do my own thing, but to do Your thing. For it is not my life but Yours—lived out in me. In the strong name of Jesus Christ. Amen.

Why do I feel so guilty, God?

GOD RESPONDS—

On Forgiving

You said you would forgive
but never forget
what that person had done
But I forgave a wandering people
many, many times
and even those who killed My Son
on a cross
I who through Isaiah promised
to blot out your sin
and no longer remember it
call you to forgive others
and to forget
and more often than
490 times
Isaiah 43:25   Mark 11:26

Good News, Not Bad

Do you know
the most important message

in My Word?
It was the prophets' first call
and My Son's last charge
to his disciples
It was that
because He suffered
and was raised on
the third day
the message should be sent out
to all nations
to repent and receive
the forgiveness of sins
Note that the emphasis
is not on your sins
but on My forgiveness
That's Good News
not bad

Joel 2:13   Micah 7:18   Luke 24:46-48   Acts 3:19

The Big Fight

You were so absorbed
in quarreling
with your spouse
that your forgot
I was watching
Aren't you ashamed
of your self-centeredness?
You won the argument
but lost the peace
Remember
I don't forgive
if you don't

So why not take
the initiative
for reconciliation?
I will give you
the courage
to do it
Colossians 3:13   Mark 11:26   Matthew 21:22

You Can't Fool Me

Let's get
one thing straight
It's not your sin
that does you in
but when you cling to it
hide it
rationalize it
and when you don't come
to the cross
and ask forgiveness for it
You see
you can't fool God!
But Good News is coming
You don't have to!
I have paid for your sin
The price was
My Son's life
So don't play games
with Me
I know your thoughts
Confess and repent
I wish not to destroy
but to forgive you

Glorify Me
in your body and your spirit
for they
are Mine
1 Corinthians 6:20

For You

My Son
Jesus Christ
died for your sins
I have kept
My promise
1 Corinthians 15:3   2 Corinthians 5:14-15
Hebrews 9:28   1 Peter 3:18

Prayer

Lord, keep reminding me that Your charge is
to declare not just repentance *and* forgiveness
but repentance *for* forgiveness. For You do not
desire my destruction nor do You want me to be
filled with guilt. But You want to *forgive* me—all
of me. So, Lord, grant me a truly penitent heart.
In the strong name of Jesus Christ. Amen.

THE CHRISTIAN ASKS—

How can I get a fresh start, God?

GOD RESPONDS—

Back to the Drawing Board

Your dreams have evaporated
Your hopes are now ashes
The castle you built in your mind
lies in ruins
Never mind
I had a grand design once, too
Then the picture window of My love
was cracked
and broken
But I devised a new plan
a new creation
Give Me your brokenness
give me your failure, your despair
and I will mend and heal
I will give you
beauty for ashes
The oil of joy
for mourning
the garment of praise

for the spirit of heaviness
For I am
the divine architect
And I make things
better than before
Try Me and see
2 Corinthians 5:17   Isaiah 61:3

Dining on Garbage

Your thoughts
haven't been very clean lately
have they?
Why do you enjoy
dining on garbage?
Soaking the tastebuds of your mind
in filth?
Come, taste and see
that I am good
Savor the sincere milk
of My Word
Have you read your Bible lately?
In what you see and read
I call you to concentrate
on things
true and noble and right
and pure and lovely and honorable
Will you
change your mind
for Me?
1 Peter 2:2   Philippians 4:8

Worship

Do you worship Me
often?
At break of day?
At sunset?
With your fellow Christians?
With every vital breath?
In the place
I have prepared for you
worship will be
your chief activity
in a joyous dimension
you cannot now imagine
That being the case
you'd better get going on it
now
John 14:2-3

Noise!

I just heard you complaining
about the noise
of the planes flying overhead
and the cars and buses outside
or the lawn mower or the vacuum cleaner
or the dishwasher
Do you want them
or don't you?
I could have let you
be born
in another age
when it took a day

to go twelve miles
in a covered wagon
or months
on a ship at sea
to reach your destination
I have let you discover
many of My mysteries
My blessings
My gifts
You can complain about them
and misuse them
or use them and
be thankful
for them
Ephesians 5:20   Philippians 4:11

Living in a Vacuum

A baby will die
without food
A plant will wither
without nourishment
So why do you feel
you will continue to grow
spiritually
if you are not regularly
in My house
to worship?
Church walls don't make
a Christian
to be sure
but neither do Christians
remain alive

much less grow
without spiritual food: My Word
and the cross-pollination
of other Christians
A coal out of the fire
alone on the hearth
dies
You can't be a Christian
in a vacuum
1 Peter 2:2   Hebrews 10:24-25

Groaning Pains

Does it hurt when I
snip off your dead branches
so that more fruit
may grow?
Do you feel pain when
My sculptor's hands
cut off your edges
which are sharp
and useless?
You may groan
you may cry
But I see
the finished product
For I am the gardener
the sculptor
your creator
Trust Me
Know that I will not
allow more pain
than you can bear

Learn more and more
to think of yourself
as a receiver
of Me
John 5:1-2   Romans 9:21   1 Corinthians 10:13

Like a Child

He said he never knew
what the apostle Paul meant
until he became a father
and at night
had to put away
childish things
That's true
When you mature
do the same
with one exception
do not put away
a childlike faith
My Son said
"Except you come to Me
as a child
with a child's faith
trusting innocent loyal
you cannot be
in My family
For of such
is My kingdom:
children "
1 Corinthians 13:11   Luke 18:16-17

Flying Like an Eagle

Are you earthbound
when you could be soaring?
Or do you get tired
while jogging?
If you are faint
and weary
tired and worn out
even in the strength
of your youth
I can give you enough power
to fly like an eagle
and run
without ever stopping
For I
I am the Source
of your strength
and I
never get tired
Isaiah 40:28-31

Useless Love

Do you do good things
because it pays off or
because you've got an eye on
what's in it for you?
That's a prostitution
of love
Do you share your
joy interest
understanding knowledge

humor   sadness
weakness or strength
out of concern for others'
life and growth?
Never exploiting
always selfless
not wanting the other to be
something you've planned
but to be
what that person must be?
True love is freeing
It serves
no utilitarian purpose
In a sense it must be
useless
to be genuine [6] [5]
1 Corinthians 13:5   John 8:36

Prayer

Almighty God, You are the beginning and
ending of all things; give me new beginnings
today. What is old make new, what is stale make
fresh. Make me ready to receive Your will. Make
today different—*You* making the difference! In
the strong name of Jesus Christ. Amen.

THE CHRISTIAN ASKS—

Am I doing O.K., God?

GOD RESPONDS—

Fork in the Road

Don't think
I never get angry
I punish
and I destroy
I am the Lord
That is My Name
My glory
I will not give
to another
But I don't desire
your punishment
or your death
I know the thoughts
I think towards you
thoughts of peace
and not of evil
So turn from
your own way
Walk in My path
and I will lead you

in a way
everlasting

Isaiah 42:8, 14   Ezekiel 33:11
Jeremiah 29:11   Psalm 139:24

R & R

I didn't say
you had to work
all the time
My Son's ministry
lasted only three years
Of course it ended
for another reason
but He took time
to rest and pray
up in the mountains
or in the desert
or by the seashore
So don't feel guilty
when you take time
to restore your body
mind and soul
Now don't get Me wrong
Work while it is day
and then one day I will give you
some real rest and relaxation
with Me

Genesis 2:3   Matthew 11:18
Matthew 14:23   Mark 6:31

Glorify Me

I heard someone down there say
they thought glorifying Me
was a waste of time
But listen to Me
I am the Lord
that is My name
and My glory I will not give
to another
nor My praise
to the little gods
you prefer
I love you
I made you
and I require your worship
and undivided obedience
Sometimes
I can be patient
just so long

Exodus 20:2-5   Isaiah 42:8
Matthew 4:10   Psalm 86:12

No Deals with Me

I heard someone say
that if I would grant her wish
she would be in church every day
the rest of her life
But I don't work that way
Our relationship must be
unconditional
You don't make promises to Me

so that I will keep a promise
You don't make deals with Me
for I have already dealt with you
through My Son
That love for you is
unconditional
That's a promise
Ephesians 2:8-9   John 15:3-5

Pride/Humility

I have good eyesight
I can see a proud person
from quite a distance
I am going to resist
and bring that person down
On the other hand
I will lift up the one
who is humble
and who has a contrite heart
and who trembles
at My Word
I have great respect for that person
and I will give that one
My grace
So make sure
you are truly humble
and not just that
you have so much
to be humble about
1 Peter 5:5   Psalm 138:6   Luke 14:11   Isaiah 66:2

On Being a Fool

If beyond the world which
you so often see as
mundane routine senseless and tragic
you have discovered
that I am madly insanely
in love with you
then don't just describe
My love to others
but share it
Be as good to others
as you have experienced
My goodness to you
You may make a fool
of yourself
in your awkward enthusiasm
but what is more fun
than being a fool
for Me? [1]
Galatians 6:9-10   1 Corinthians 4:10

How Important Are You?

Do you take yourself
pretty seriously?
Your career?
Your time schedule?
Your own importance?
Or do you take time
for others
To be actively helpful

in trifling things
The meanest services?
Your schedule is not
your own
It is Mine
to arrange
Only where your hands
are not too good
for little deeds
of love and mercy
in everyday helpfulness
can your mouth
joyfully and convincingly
proclaim My love
and mercy [3]
Galatians 6:9-10   Luke 6:36

Just a Little Bit More

You say things are going
pretty well for you
these days
and that you love Me
and have been serving Me
I appreciate that
But I have a question
Are you really doing all you can
in My employ?
Are you a spiritual resource
to others?
Is your potential
for My kindgom

fully released?
Have you dared to risk
everything
for Me?
Remember
to whom more is given
more is required
1 Peter 4:7-10   Romans 12:13
1 Timothy 6:17-19   Luke 12:48

The Secret of Contentment

Do you complain
or grumble
about your circumstances?
Learn the secret from Brother Paul
how to get along happily
whether you have much
or little
Learn how anywhere anytime
to be content
to be satisfied
with what you have
I give the power
through My Son
to live that way
That doesn't mean
not to work
for if you don't
you won't eat
So live a quiet life
mind your own business
earn your own living

and I promise you
contentment
Philippians 4:11   John 9:4   2 Thessalonians 3:10
1 Thessalonians 4:11

No Other Plans

Did you ever think
of your feet hands and voice
as being Mine?
Not just that
you are My creation
but My servant?
I depend on you
to carry out
My business
For when My Son returned to heaven
and the angels expressed surprise
that He had left
the work of My kingdom
in the hands of
just a few disciples
He simply told them
We had
no other plans
Matthew 22:37   John 9:4

True Sharing

Did you say
you really wanted to share

what you have
with others?
Are you willing to do that
without clarifying
your superior position
so that others will know
what you gave?
Are you willing to change
your life-style?
That would be
true sharing
Are you willing to be
poorer than before?
That would be
true sharing
You say you really want
to share?
Blessed are those
who having dreamed dreams
are compelled
to make them come true [10]
Matthew 19:21   Luke 6:38

Prayer

Crush my pride in my achievements, Lord.
Remind me not to take Your mercy and patience
lightly. Guide me to find the proper balance
between leisure and labor. Help me to live and
work for Your glory and honor, not my own. In
the strong name of Jesus Christ. Amen.

THE CHRISTIAN ASKS—

Why don't I understand You, God?

GOD RESPONDS—

Rejected

I know
how you are hurting right now
I have known hurt too
Adam and Eve hid from Me
Cain lied to Me
Moses disappointed Me
Jonah fled from Me
I could go on
indeed, all My people forsook Me
Then I sent My Son
My only Son
and they killed Him
I hurt too
I know rejection
Even though
you my child some days
live as if I do not exist
and that hurts Me
I forgive you
I love you

Know now that you are not alone
Others may forsake you but
I am with you
always
Isaiah 53:3

Not My Will

I'm truly sorry
that child died
Don't say
it was "God's will,"
or that I
"Called him home "
True, he is at peace now
here with Me
But Death is your enemy
and Mine
I did not will it
It came on all mankind
for all have sinned
and not sooner for some
because they sinned more
If you ask
where I was
when that child died
I was at the same place
as that day
My Son died
on Calvary
2 Peter 3:9   Romans 5:12

They Never Had a Chance

Do you sometimes wonder
whether I am a fair and loving God
when you think of millions of people
in distant lands
who have never heard of Me
who "never had a chance"?
Well, don't question My integrity
or try to fathom My mind
Are you My counselor?
Do I owe you explanations?
If you are really concerned
are you getting My message to them
If not yourself
through missionaries?
So don't question what happens to people
who haven't heard about Me
That's My business
and I can
handle it
But I have revealed
Myself to you
That's your concern
How do you
handle that?
Romans 11:33-36   Romans 10:14-15

You Can't Wiggle Your Finger

Did you think
it was an act of your will
to believe in Me?

76

You didn't choose Me
but I chose you
You can turn away from Me
but you can't turn to Me
You say that
that isn't logical
But you can't fathom
the mystery of conversion
Just remember
you were a spiritual corpse
couldn't even wiggle
your little finger
in My direction
but I called you
through My Word
Broke your heart
Drew you to Me
Forgave your sin
And kindled the spark
of faith
through My Spirit

John 15:16   Ephesians 2:8-9
Galatians 4:6   Titus 3:5-7

Shut Your Mouth!

Do you sometimes wonder
why things go wrong
and you suffer
seemingly without reason
even though you
believe in Me?
Learn from Job

He had the same problem
He asked why I was testing him
He tried to instruct Me
But he was asking
the wrong questions
Well, I asked him
a few questions . . .
like where he was
when I created all things
Job needed reminding
as you do
that you are the creature
and I am the Creator
I AM GOD
And there's a time
like Job
when you need
to put your hand
over your mouth
in silence
and say nothing

Job 10:2   Job 40:2   Job 38-40
Job 40:4   Job 37:23

The Chain Reaction

Do you want to know how
to be joyful
even in the middle of
trials and troubles?
Here's My promise:
when you suffer
know that from that experience

can come patient endurance
that in turn will develop
a mature character
which brings My approval
From My approval
comes a steady hope
which will never disappoint you
For at that point
I send My Spirit
as a present
flooding My love
into your heart
That gives you the power
to be joyful
even when you suffer
It's quite a chain reaction
isn't it? 4
Romans 5:3-5

Patience!

Look back
in your life
Don't you think
I've been pretty patient
with you at times?
How are you doing
in being patient
with others around you?
I call you to
be patient with all
I will give you the power
the mercy, and compassion

to do it
or My name isn't God
Or do you want Me
to stop being patient
with you?
1 Thessalonians 5:14   Hebrews 10:36   James 5:11

The Gift-Giver

Are you disappointed
because you haven't enjoyed
the spiritual experience
a friend has had?
You prayed
and sought Me
but it didn't happen
But don't put a specification
on My Spirit
You may want a vision
and get a fact
You may want emotion
and receive conviction
Rather than ecstasy
I may give you
a quieter joy
which flows from
your steady faith
in Me
So don't dictate
to My Spirit
but remain open
to whatever He gives
For while He is quite

unpredictable
He does
give gifts [8]
1 Corinthians 12:1, 4-11   John 3:8

You Are Tired

I know
you just can't believe
he's gone
Well, I will tell you
how it happened
He and I used to take
long walks together
and one day I noticed
he was especially tired
So I said
"Why don't you come
and stay at My house
and rest awhile?"
He thought
that was a pretty good idea
so he did
Now he's at My house
and you can visit him there
for one day
I will ask *you*
If you would like to take
a long walk
with Me
Genesis 5:24   John 14:3

They Don't Remember You

Don't get angry with Me
because your loved one died
Be angry at death
That's the Enemy
Meanwhile realize that
your beloved
is no longer aware of you
so supremely happy is that person
in My presence
Your loved one is spared
the evils to come
and utterly at peace
and rest
The hard work
is over
Shouldn't that
comfort you?
So be patient
You will see each other
again
And although you
weep now
joy will come
in the morning

Isaiah 63:16   Revelation 14:13
Isaiah 57:2   Psalm 30:5

Prayer

I don't always understand You, God, but I am
beginning to see how much You love me. I truly
want to love You. Please send Your Holy Spirit

into my heart that I may respond faithfully to
Your call. In the strong name of Jesus Christ.
Amen.

Why am I so afraid, God?

GOD RESPONDS—

Behind the Curtain

While you were asleep
I was watching over you
I was glad when you
pushed back the bedroom curtains
and said
"Good morning, Lord!
Thank you for another day "
And for the way you said
the other night
"Perhaps tonight, Lord?"
I'm glad you are ready
watching and praying
as I have told you to be
For I will come
when you least expect Me
Meanwhile, don't live in fear
for My love, which is perfect
casts out fear
Be on the lookout for Me
It will be a joyous meeting
Now I am still
behind that curtain

but then
you will see Me
face to face
Psalm 121:4   Lamentations 3:22-23   Mark 13:33
Matthew 24:42   1 John 4:18   1 Corinthians 13:12

No Campaign Promise

Do You despair
because your nation
is plagued by war
or drought or famine
or political turmoil?
I have a promise
for you
If My people
called by My Name
will humble themselves
and pray
and search for Me
and turn from their wicked ways
I will hear them
forgive their sin
and heal their land
That's not just
a campaign promise
2 Chronicles 7:14

Calm Down

Worry is interest

paid on trouble
before it falls due
So don't worry
but pray
And thank Me
for My answers
Do you know
what will happen?
You will experience
My peace
which will
calm your mind
My peace
will keep your heart
quiet and at rest
as you trust
in My Son
Philippians 4:6-7

The Storm to Come

Did you ever notice
how restless animals are
before a storm
or an earthquake?
The whole creation
groans and trembles
till My coming
You too should groan
and wait patiently
for Me
Do not fear
but wait in hope

and soon you shall see Me
face to face
Romans 8:22-25   1 Corinthians 13:12

Nothing Happened

Your friend commented
on how he just missed
having a tragic accident
and what a sign that was
of My protection
That's true
But I'll give you
an even greater demonstration
of My care
Nothing
absolutely nothing
even came near
hurting you today
Now isn't that
even more
fantastic?
Isaiah 26:3

Prayer

Take hold of my hand, Lord. I'm afraid. Put
Your peace in my heart, the peace I can't create
on my own and which is so absent in the world
around me. *Your* peace, Lord! In the strong name
of Jesus Christ. Amen.

THE CHRISTIAN ASKS—

What else do I need to hear, God?

GOD RESPONDS—

Whose Side Are You On?

You think you've
got it made
because your salvation
is a free gift from Me?
It is
But there is no freedom
without responsibility
and that freedom
being tested
If you think you're standing
on pretty solid ground
be careful
lest you fall
If things are going
pretty well for you
maybe you're in the enemy's camp
and not Mine
For whom I love
I test
but I also provide you the strength

to overcome
and so to bear the mark
of being My child
and My disciple
John 8:36   1 Corinthians 10:12-13   Hebrews 12:5-8

Giving

Don't give to Me
because you think
I need your gift
but rather
because you need
to give
Give because it is your nature
to give
Give because
you need
the spiritual exercise
Give because
you are an imitator of Me
I gave you
everything
Philippians 4:17   Luke 6:38   2 Corinthians 9:7

Hand it Over!

It's not so much of your money
or your work that I want
I want you
all of you

I don't come to torment
your natural self
but to kill it
I don't just want a branch off
I want the whole tree down
I don't want
to drill the tooth
or crown it
but have it out
Hand over
the whole outfit
and I will give you
a new self
In fact
I will give you
My self
and My own will
shall become
yours [11]
Mark 8:35   Romans 6:1-11   Matthew 26:39

Color

Have you ever felt superior
to someone
of another color?
Didn't you know
that I
am color-blind?
In fact
it would be helpful
if you could live
in the skin

of a person with a color
different from your own
so you could feel
the nail-prints
in that person's palms
Acts 10:34   Romans 10:12

The Bread of Loneliness

You say you are concerned
about the suffering
in the world
I hope that isn't
just talk
for you cannot embrace
a broken world
without being broken yourself
You cannot feel pity
for the hungry
until you have *been* hungry
You cannot feel sorrow
for the lonely
until you have eaten
the bread of loneliness
Don't just talk
about the pain of others
until you have felt
that pain
Take a lesson
from My Son
No one had ever spoken
like He did

But words weren't enough
He acted
1 John 3:18   John 7:46   Hebrews 4:15
Philippians 2:5-8

Youth/Aging

Your age
means nothing to Me
except that
if you are young
you shouldn't let others
look down on you
Be an example to them
in all you do
If you are old
don't glorify the time
when you were young
but glorify Me
for I will carry you
and bear you
and deliver you
and cause you
to bear fruit
in your old age
So remember
your age
means nothing to Me
We don't celebrate birthdays
up here
in heaven
Psalm 39:4-7   1 Timothy 4:12   Isaiah 46:4
Psalm 92:4   Psalm 71:9

Love of the World?

I never said
not to love the world
as My good creation
but I did say
not to fall in love
with evil things which divert
your love from Me
Your self's desires
what you see and want
the things people are
so proud of
Those are all misdirected
Rather enjoy My creation
but focus your real desires
on My desires for you
and I promise
you will live
forever
1 John 2:15   Matthew 6:19-21   John 3:16

Weeping and Laughing

I want you to laugh
at times
but there is a time to laugh
and a time to weep
Even when you are laughing
your heart may sorrow
and your mirth
turn to heaviness
I laugh too

94

in derision
at the wicked
who think they are
fooling Me
as if they could
But when you hunger
for Me
you will be filled
and your weeping
will be turned
to laughter
Ecclesiastes 3:4   Proverbs 14:13   James 4:9
Psalm 2:4   Psalm 37:13   Luke 6:21

Catching God's Vision

Would you like
a surprise?
Then in your relationship
with your spouse
or a friend
seek not to be loved
nor to love the other
because you are drawn
to that person
Seek rather to
free that person and to
catch My vision
of what that person
can become
Concentrate on that
It will radically change
your relationship [7]
2 Corinthians 5:17

Why Not?

I heard
he wanted her
to sleep with him
before they were married
She did not give him
pious phrases
but said she couldn't
because of Me
When he said
"What has He ever done for you?"
she simply replied (concerning herself)
"I exist "
That was
a pretty good
answer
1 Corinthians 6:19-20

Going Around Only Once

I know some of you
are in great pain
and ready to die
but have courage
The hour
has not yet come
On the other hand
I wish some others of you
would take a lesson
from the apostle Paul:
mixed feelings
wanting to be with Me

yet ready to stay and work
So be prepared to die
but find the balance
to live with zest and vividness
satisfaction and detachment
at the same time
for you only go around
once
A question then
Are you ready to die
Or afraid to live?
Philippians 1:23-26   Matthew 10:28

Wrong Address

That address
on your driver's license
is misleading
Your real residence
is in one of the
numberless mansions
up here
Don't fall in love
with that island colony
of Mine
down there
for you are only
passing through
You are
a stranger a pilgrim
a foreigner a refugee
an itinerant a visitor
Concentrate on that

kind of thinking
and you won't forget
your correct address
Philippians 3:20   Hebrews 11:13

Sowing Wild Oats

Don't kid yourself
You sowed wild oats
and expected
a healthy crop?
I have set down
a pretty basic law
What you sow
you reap
You get exactly
what you plant
You may deceive yourself
for a while
but you'll never
make a fool
of Me
Galatians 6:7-9   Matthew 7:16-20   James 3:12

The Skeleton in the Closet

You asked Me
to come in to
the house of your life
and stay with you
but you refused

to give up
that stinking closet
on the second floor
Some rotten garbage
you wanted to hang on to
Well, give Me the key
to that closet
and let Me take over
the whole works
or I'm going to take
My bed
out on
the back porch [9]
John 14:23   Matthew 22:37

This Program Was Made Possible

Can you imagine
what it's like
to live forever?
I know what it's like
It's great
It'll be wonderful
having you up here
with Me
I have a place
all set up for you
This program
was made possible
by My Son's death
and resurrection
When you
believe in Him

even though you die
you will live again
Isn't that fantastic?
So remember
And don't doubt it
Because I live forever
you will live forever
It's as certain
as that

John 14:1-3   John 11:25-26   John 14:19
Romans 6:8

Footprints in the Valley

By now you have heard
many of My promises
(there are many more)
and have responded
in faith
feeling you have done
your part
and that now the next move
is up to Me
You are mistaken
You can't fly across
the valley of the shadow
you must walk
the rocky path
step by step
But you are not alone
on your journey
There are always footprints
ahead of you

in the valley of the shadow
They are Mine
Come
let's walk
together [12]
Psalm 23:4

Prayer

I thank You for all Your promises, Lord!
Now, great Promiser, fill me with Your Spirit!
Make me a receiver of Your will! Mold me, shape
me, use me, Lord! In the strong name of Jesus
Christ! Amen.

Epilogue

Imagine you are walking on a suburban street and see three little children, all under the age of five, in the back of a station wagon. The luggage rack on top of the car is loaded with baggage. The father is just closing the garage door, the mother shutting the front door. It is obvious the family is leaving on a trip.

You walk up to the little children and say, "Where are you going?" Wide-eyed they stare back at you. They don't know.

"What highway are you taking?" No answer.

"Where are you going to have dinner tonight?" No response.

"Where are you going to sleep tonight?" Still no reply.

"With whom are you going?" you ask.

Their eyes light up, their faces break into smiles. "With Mommy and Daddy!" they exclaim.*

Your life lies ahead of you. There are many unknowns. For many of the questions you have, you have no answers. But you do have The Answerer with you. He has *promised* to be by your side . . . every step of the way.

Do you really need anything more?

---

*From *The Best of Your Life is the Rest of Your Life,* by the author (Nashville, Tenn.: Abingdon Press, 1977), p. 35.

Credits

1. Andrew M. Greeley, *The Great Mysteries* (New York: The Seabury Press, 1976), pp. 9—10.

2. John Powell, *A Reason to Live! A Reason to Die* (Niles, Ill.: Argus Communications, 1972), pp. 137—140.

3. Dietrich Bonhoeffer, *Life Together* (New York: Harper & Row, 1954), p. 113; pp. 99-100.

4. Margaret Wold, *The Critical Moment* (Minneapolis: Augsburg Publishing House, 1978), p. 126.

5. Anthony T Padovano, *The Estranged God* (New York: Sheed and Ward, 1966), p. 177 and p. 166.

6. William Hordern, *Living By Grace* (Philadelphia: Westminster Press, 1975), p. 157.

7. Peter A. Bertocci, "What Makes a Christian Home?" *(The Christian Century,* May 6, 1959).

8. Catherine Marshall, *Something More* (New York: Avon Books, 1976), pp. 242-243.

9. Robert Boyd Munger, "My Heart Christ's Home," a tract from the Billy Graham Evangelistic Association, Box 779, Minneapolis, Minn. 55440.

10. Manas Buthelezi, clergyman, South Africa.

11. C. S. Lewis, *Beyond Personality* (New York: The Macmillan Company, 1947), p. 40.

12. Catherine Marshall, *To Live Again* (New York: Avon Books, 1972), p. 113.